DATE DUE

Demco, Inc. 38-293

Plant Reproduction

Richard & Louise Spilsbury

Heinemann Library
Chicago, Illinois

Customer Service 888-454-2279
Visit our website at www.heinemannlibrary.com

Designed by Macwiz
Illustrated by Jeff Edwards
Originated by Ambassador Litho Ltd
Printed by Wing King Tong, Hong Kong

07 06 05 04 03
10 9 8 7 6 5 4 3 2 1

Library of Congress Cataloging-in-Publication Data
Spilsbury, Louise.
   Plant reproduction / Louise and Richard Spilsbury.
       v. cm. -- (Life of plants)
Includes bibliographical references (p.   ).
Contents: What is reproduction? -- Reproducing with seeds -- What flowers do -- Pollination -- How does insect pollination work? -- Attracting animal pollinators -- Pollen dispersal by wind -- When does pollination happen? -- Fertilization -- Conifers -- Seeds -- Kinds of seeds -- Seed dispersal: wind and water -- Seed dispersal: fruit and nuts -- Other ways of dispersing seeds -- Reproducing with spores -- Other ways of reproducing -- Reproducing from underground -- Try it yourself! -- Facts and figures.
   ISBN 1-4034-0298-1 (HC)   1-4034-0506-9 (PB)
   1. Plants--Reproduction--Juvenile literature. [1. Plants--Reproduction.] I. Spilsbury, Richard, 1963- II. Title.
   QK825 .S65 2002
   575.6--dc21
                    2001008305

Acknowledgments
The author and publishers are grateful to the following for permission to reproduce copyright material: pp. 4, 5, 6, 8, 10, 11, 15, 16, 17, 18, 21, 26, 28, 29, 36, 39 Holt Studios; pp. 7, 13, 19, 24, 32 FLPA; pp. 9, 12, 14, 22, 25, 27, 30, 31, 33, 34, 37, 38 Oxford Scientific Films; p. 23 Science Photo Library: Adrienne Hart-Davis.

Cover photograph reproduced with permission of Holt Studios.

Every effort has been made to contact copyright holders of any material reproduced in this book. Any omissions will be rectified in subsequent printings if notice is given to the publisher.

Some words are shown in bold, **like this.** You can find out what they mean by looking in the glossary.

Contents

A plant may be called different things in different countries, so every type of plant has a Latin name that can be recognized anywhere in the world. Latin names are made of two words—the first is the **genus,** or general, group a plant belongs to and the second is its **species,** or specific, name. Latin plant names are given in brackets throughout this book.

What Is Reproduction?

Every living thing on Earth, from the smallest insect to the largest tree, is here because of **reproduction.** Reproduction is the way plants and animals produce young that grow into new plants and animals that look like themselves. In the animal kingdom, cats produce kittens that grow into adult cats, and frogs produce eggs that hatch into tadpoles, which grow into frogs. In the plant kingdom, oak trees produce acorns that grow into new oak trees, and potato plants produce potatoes that grow into new potato plants.

Why do plants reproduce?

All **organisms** gradually become older and eventually die. Some plants, such as the poppy, live only for a few months. Others, such as the yew tree, can live for thousands of years. If these plants did not reproduce and make other living things like themselves before they died, their **species** would die out.

◄ The ancestors of these horsetail plants were the giant horsetails that first grew on Earth nearly 400 million years ago.

Kinds of reproduction

Plants use two kinds of reproduction: **sexual reproduction** and **asexual reproduction**. In sexual reproduction, a young plant has two parent plants. Plants that reproduce in this way, such as sunflowers and oak trees, make **seeds**. The seeds can then grow into new plants. When these young plants are full grown, they will produce seeds that will grow into new plants themselves. The majority of plants in the world make new plants by means of sexual reproduction.

Some plants, such as strawberry and potato plants, use asexual reproduction in addition to or instead of sexual reproduction. Asexual reproduction involves only one parent plant. One way of reproducing asexually is when a small part of the parent plant, such as a piece of **root** or **stem**, grows into a new plant. When this new plant is big enough, it breaks away from the parent plant and becomes a separate individual, able to live and produce new young plants of its own. Some plants, such as ferns, reproduce asexually by means of **spores**.

▲ These **saplings** have grown from seeds that dropped from the trees above.

Sexual Reproduction in Plants

A **seed** starts life, as all **organisms** do, as a microscopic living part called a **cell.** Cells are the tiny building blocks that make up all living things. Plants, like many other organisms, have many different types of cells in the different parts of their bodies. For example, some cells are specialized to carry water around the plant, while others are specialized to make food by **photosynthesis.** The cells required for **sexual reproduction** are called **sex cells.** Organisms make sex cells in their male or female parts.

How does reproduction happen?

In the first stage of sexual reproduction, a sex cell from the male parts of an organism and a sex cell from the female parts of another organism have to join. The new cell then divides many times, increasing in number to make an **embryo,** a very early form of the new living thing. In plants, the embryo develops inside a seed. The seed forms inside the female parts of a plant. When the seeds are fully formed, the plant lets them go.

◄ These are the seeds growing at the top of wheat plants. People grow wheat for its seeds, which can be made into bread and other foods.

Making a difference

Why do so many plants make seeds when they could simply split off a part of themselves to create a new plant? It has everything to do with being different.

Inside each sex cell there are bits of information called **genes.** Genes are like tiny instruction manuals. They control not only how an organism looks but also how it will survive, grow, and change throughout its life. When two sex cells join, they mix together two sets of genes, one from each parent. As a result, the embryo ends up with its own unique mixture of genes. It is almost like a recipe in which the ingredients are mixed together to create something new.

When a plant grows from a seed, it will be similar to its parent plants, but it will also be slightly different from both of them. These tiny differences may improve its chances of survival. When a plant makes a new plant from a part of itself, however, the new plant has the same genes and is exactly the same as its parent. This new plant will be no better at growing and surviving than its parent.

► This poppy grew from a seed. It looks almost identical to its parent plants, but it may have subtle differences in its genes that help it to survive and thrive better than its parents.

What Flowers Do

Flowers are the special parts of a plant where **seeds** are made. When you look at most flowers, the parts that catch your eye are the colorful and often large **petals.** You have to look more closely to see the parts that do the real work. They are tucked away in the center of the flower, where there are female and male parts that produce seeds that can grow into new plants.

Female part

The female part is usually found in the very center of the flower. It is called the **pistil.** The pistil consists of three parts—the **ovary, style,** and **stigma.** The ovary is the swollen or rounded part at the bottom of the pistil. This is where the seeds are produced. The ovary contains one or more female **sex cells** called **ovules.** The ovules are the parts that can develop into seeds. The stigma is at the top of the pistil. It has a pointed or flattened end that is usually sticky. The style is a single large stalk that attaches the ovary to the stigma.

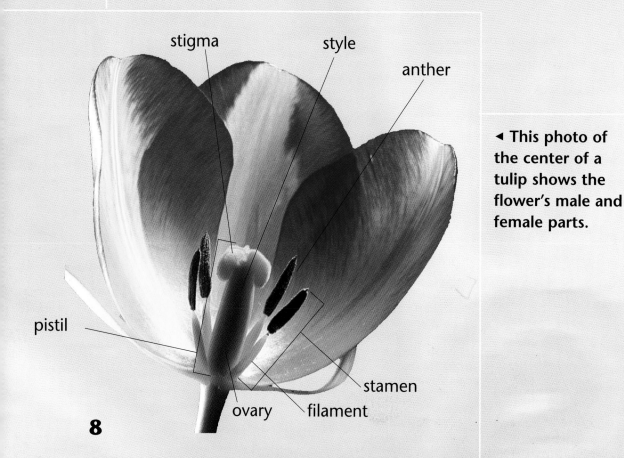

stigma

style

anther

pistil

ovary

filament

stamen

◄ **This photo of the center of a tulip shows the flower's male and female parts.**

Male part

The male part of a flower is called the **stamen.** Each stamen is made up of an **anther** and a **filament.** The anther is the enlarged tip of the stamen. It is like a special bag that produces and holds **pollen** grains. Pollen grains contain the plant's male sex cells. The filament is the part of the stamen that supports the anther. Some types of flowers have a few stamens, while others have many.

Different kinds of flowers

Most flowering plants, such as the tulip shown opposite, make flowers that contain both male and female parts. Some plants make two different flowers—some with only female parts, others with only male parts. In some plants, such as oak (*Quercus*) and hazelnut (*Corylus*), both male and female flowers appear on the same plant. In other kinds, such as holly and fig trees, a single plant has either all male or all female flowers.

The secret of pollen grains

Pollen grains are so tiny—usually the size of dust particles—that we never really see what individual grains look like. The only way to see a pollen grain is with the help of a microscope that enlarges the image many times. Up close, you can see that each type of plant has its own individual kind of pollen grain. Pollen grains may look like spiky balls, doughnuts, coffee beans, or sponges. Some even have hairs!

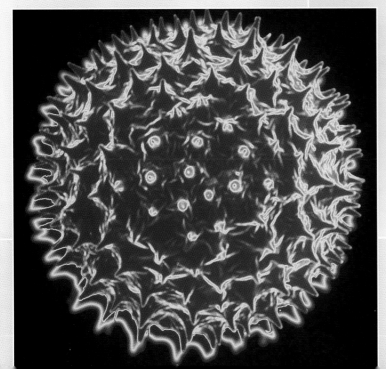

◄ This is a pollen grain from a mallow plant.

What Is Pollination?

Pollination is the first stage in the process of **seed** production. Before an **ovule** can become a seed, it has to join with the **pollen** of the same or another flower. Pollination is when pollen travels from the **stamens** to the **pistils** of the same plant or a different plant of the same kind.

Pollen clues

Pollen grains are hardy, so they don't get damaged as they move from one flower to another. They are so tough that they can survive for many years. Scientists have used pollen grains preserved in marshy ground called **peat bogs** to figure out what plants were growing on Earth thousands of years ago.

◄ The petals of the bottlebrush (*Callistemon*) plant are very small and pale. It is the long, bright-red stamens that put on the real show. They give the flowers the appearance of the kind of brushes used to clean bottles.

Pollen grains are produced in the **anthers** at the top of the stamen. When a plant's pollen is ready, the anthers open by splitting down the middle. The two sides curl back to expose and release the pollen. So how does the pollen move? Because they cannot move from place to place to pass on their pollen, they have other ways of doing it. The two main methods of moving pollen are by wind and by insects. We will look at these ways of pollination in more detail later in the book.

Cross-pollination

Most flowers are designed to **disperse** pollen from one plant to another plant of the same kind. The pollen is moved from the male parts of one flower to the female parts of another flower on a separate plant. This is called cross-pollination. Seeds made by plants using cross-pollination contain **genes** from two parents. Remember, a mixture of genes means new plants will have some of the features of each parent. But they will also have some unique features that might help them survive in places their parents could not.

Many plants have ways of making sure that only cross-pollination occurs. A willow tree (*Salix*) has either all female or all male flowers, and the stamens of flowers on a saxifrage (*Saxifraga*) plant die before the **stigmas** have developed. The plant can be pollinated only by the pollen from a separate plant.

Self-pollination

Many plants are also able to self-pollinate. This means that the pollen from the stamen of a flower reaches the stigma of the very same flower. Plants often use this do-it-yourself technique when they no longer have a chance to cross-pollinate. Honeysuckle (*Lonicera*) flowers, for example, have stigmas that are held away from the anthers so that self-pollination is unlikely. But toward the end of the flowering period, if cross-pollination has not occurred, the stigma droops down among the anthers to self-pollinate.

▶ **At the end of their flowering time, the stigmas on honeysuckle flowers droop down and take up pollen from their own anthers.**

anthers   stigma

Pollination in Action

On spring and summer days, you can usually see bees flying from one brightly colored flower to another. If you keep watching, you may notice that they tend to visit the same kinds of flowers. When you see this happening, you are watching **pollination** in action!

Pollen deliveries

Bees, butterflies, flies, and midges are like living delivery trucks for plants that use insects to pollinate their flowers. The **pollen** these plants produce is slightly stickier, rougher, or larger than pollen made by plants that use wind for pollination. When an insect lands on one of their flowers, the sticky pollen grains attach themselves to the insect's body or legs. When the insect flies off, it carries the pollen load with it. When it lands on another flower, the pollen brushes off again. If it brushes off onto the **stigma** of this next flower, then pollination has been successful.

Insects visit the flowers to eat a sweet-tasting liquid called **nectar,** which is stored at the base of the **petals.** The position of the nectar source is important. To get to it, insects have to brush past the **anthers.** When they do so, pollen sticks to them.

▶ As the bee dines on this flower's nectar, pollen is showered onto its back. When it lands on the next flower, the pollen rubs off onto the stigma.

Pollen pantry

Some flowers that are pollinated by insects do not produce nectar. Instead, their pollen is a **nutritious** food for insects. The poppy flower has lots of **stamens** that form its distinctive black center. These stamens make plenty of pollen—its insect visitors eat some of it and transfer some of it when they move to another flower.

Animal antics

In some places, birds and other animals help to pollinate plants as well. As hummingbirds poke their long beaks into hibiscus flowers to drink nectar, pollen brushes onto their head.

In North American deserts, birds pollinate the saguaro cactus (*Cereus giganteus*) by day, and bats do the night shift!

▶ In Australia, the small honey opossum lives entirely on nectar and pollen that it licks from flowers using its long tongue.

Flower shapes

Most flower shapes are designed to ensure that insects can land easily on them and that they always rub against the anthers when they visit. Some flowers grow close together in groups called **clusters.** Clusters form a platform that makes it easy for insects to land. Other flowers have petals that form tubes into which insects must crawl to get the pollen or nectar. Take a good look at flowers next time you are out and see if you can tell how their shapes help them to be pollinated.

Attracting Insect Pollinators

How do insects know which flowers to visit and when? The answer is that flowers use their colorful **petals** and sweet scents to entice their **pollinators.** Their red, yellow, blue, and purple flowers are like advertisements, telling their insect customers that they have **nectar** to offer. The petals produce their sweetest and strongest scents when the **pollen** is ready because this is the time when they most need to attract the insects.

Some insects, such as bumblebees, butterflies, and hoverflies, **pollinate** a variety of flowers. Other flowers are pollinated only by certain kinds of insects. For example, some flowers use flies for pollination. Flies usually feed on dead and rotting material, so sweet-smelling flowers do not attract them. Instead, these plants often have flowers that smell like decaying flesh.

▲ This eucera bee has landed on a bee orchid and will help pollinate it.

Masters of disguise

To make sure they are pollinated, bee orchids (*Lycaste barringtoniae*) have become experts at disguise! These plants produce flowers that look and smell like a female eucera bee. The disguise is so convincing that the male eucera bee is tricked into thinking the flower really is a female bee. When he lands on the flower, the pollen rubs off on his head. He flies off again, only to be attracted to another bee orchid. When he lands on the next flower, the pollen rubs off onto its **stigma** and pollination is complete.

Honeyguides

In addition to using scent to attract pollinators, many flowers have petals with special markings, called **honeyguides,** to show the insects the way to the nectar. These markings often take the form of bright lines that are colored differently from the rest of the petal so that they stand out. Some flowers have patterns of dots leading to the nectar source. These markings are kind of like the markings on an airport runway, guiding the insects into the correct landing position. On their way to the nectar source, the insects will almost certainly brush past the plant's **anthers** and **stigmas** and pick up or drop off pollen.

If you look closely at most flowers, you should be able to see their honeyguides. However, some honeyguides are visible only in **ultraviolet** light, which insects can see but humans cannot.

▲ In addition to petal patterns like these, in most flowers the scent gets stronger at the base of the petals. These features help lead the insects to the center of the flower where the nectar and pollen are located.

Open for business?

New flowers open on a horsechestnut tree every day during the flowering season. If you look closely, you will see that some flowers have yellow lines on the petals. These lines guide the bees into the center of the flower to find the nectar. When the nectar has run out, the lines turn red. Like a "Sold out" sign in a shop window, the red lines tell the bees when a flower has run out of nectar.

Pollen Dispersal by Wind

When you brush past grass plants in summer, you may have noticed the clouds of dust that blow off the plants. This dust is **pollen.** Plants that use the wind to help them **pollinate** their flowers include grasses and many trees and **shrubs.** Their pollen is small and light, so it is easily carried away from the **anthers** by the wind. The wind can carry pollen farther than you might think—up to about 3,000 miles (4,800 kilometers) away from parent plants in some cases.

Wind pollination is somewhat random. Plants cannot control where the wind will carry their pollen. There is only the slightest chance that a pollen grain will reach a **stigma** of the right kind of plant. So wind-pollinated flowers make incredibly large amounts of pollen. Just one birch catkin, for example, may hold over five million pollen grains. By releasing such huge amounts of pollen, wind-pollinated plants increase their chances of **reproducing.** However, much of the pollen will land on different types of plants or fall to the ground and go to waste.

◄ **The catkins that hang from the alder tree (*Alnus*) are its male flowers. On dry days, the wind blows millions of grains of pollen from the anthers. In spring, nearby rivers are covered with alder pollen.**

Plants that use wind for pollination do not need big, bright **petals** or a sweet smell to attract insects. They have small, dull-colored, unscented flowers that sometimes do not even look like flowers. The important thing about wind-pollinated flowers is that they grow where they can easily catch the breeze. Most have anthers that dangle from the ends of long stalks. Their stigmas are often large and feathery. This shape gives them a better chance of sweeping up the pollen as it blows past.

Hay fever

Most pollen is so tiny that it cannot be seen by the human eye. However, when it blows into the eyes, nose, or throat of a person with hay fever, it can cause sneezing, itchy eyes, bad headaches, and a stuffy or runny nose. Many people take medicine to control their hay fever and avoid grassy fields in summertime.

Grass flowers grow at the end of long, flexible **stems.** The stems hold the grass flowers above other plants, and they move with the wind so that the pollen is blown off easily. Flower stalks grow from the tops of the stems. When the pollen is ripe, the anther enlarges so that it dangles outside of the flower. The wind carries the pollen to the feathery stigmas of another grass plant.

◄ **Grass flowers don't have petals. They have green, leaflike scales to protect their flower parts. The photo at the left shows couch grass flowers.**

When Does Pollination Happen?

Plants do not grow flowers, nor do they produce and release **pollen** throughout the whole year. It is important that flowering and pollination happen at the correct time. Plants use up a lot of their **energy** growing flowers, and if they missed out on **pollination**, they would miss the chance to **reproduce.**

Seasons

Most plants that are pollinated by wind or insects produce and release pollen in the spring and summer months. One of the simplest reasons for this timing is to avoid the harsh winter weather. Hard rains and severe cold can damage flowers and their pollen. Also, more insects are active in spring and summer, so this is when insect-pollinated plants have a better chance of being pollinated.

▲ Some wind-pollinated trees, such as this willow (*Salix*), release pollen early in spring, before leaves cover the branches and block the wind that carries their pollen grains.

Night callers

Some flowering plants are pollinated at night. Many, such as evening primrose (*Oenothera*), are pollinated by moths that only come out in the dark. Evening primrose flowers give off their strongest, sweetest scent at night so that moths can find them easily. Many of the flowers that are pollinated at night are white or cream-colored, because these colors show up better in the dark or twilight than other colors.

An open and shut case?

Most plants are pollinated during the day. Because of this, some flowers open in the daytime and close at night. These plants use their flower **petals** to protect their pollen at night. Crocus flowers open only when it is warm and sunny. That is when the insects that pollinate them are active. At night, they close up their petals to keep the pollen safe until the next day.

Rain and even morning dew can damage pollen. For this reason, some flowers, such as the daisy, close their petals in bad weather to keep the water out. In a really bad rainy spell, they might keep their petals closed for days. Flowers whose petals hang down, such as the foxglove, are not in danger of water getting inside them, so they do not need to close their petals when it rains.

◄ Wood anemones close at night and open up when the warmth of the sun touches them.

Delaying tactics

Some plants produce flowers gradually, with some flowers appearing later than others. This gives them more time to be successfully pollinated. For example, the fireweed (*Chamerion angustifolium*) grows individual flowers on a spike. The flowers at the bottom of the spike open first. Gradually other flowers open, with those at the top opening last. Bees visit the lower flowers first and work their way up day after day until all the flowers on the spike have died.

Fertilization

Once the **pollen** from one flower has landed on the **stigma** of another flower, it is time for the next stage in the process of **seed** production—**fertilization**. Fertilization in plants happens when a male **sex cell** from a pollen grain and a female sex cell from an **ovule** join to make a seed. A flower's ovules, you remember, are inside the **ovary,** the bottom part of the **pistil** of the flower. So how does pollen travel from the top of a sticky stigma on the outside of the pistil to the inside of the ovary? The answer is that the pollen itself never makes it to the ovary!

Into the ovary

The pollen has a remarkable way of getting its sex cells into the ovary: a tube grows down from the pollen grain into the pistil. This tube passes through the stigma and down to the ovary. Then the male sex cell from the pollen grain travels down the tube. In the ovary, it joins with the ovule. The ovule has now been fertilized and can grow into a seed. In some plants this whole process takes only a few hours. In others, such as some orchids, it may take a few months.

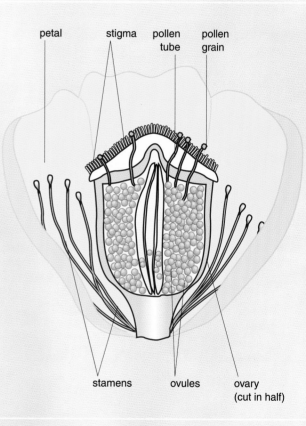

petal stigma pollen tube pollen grain

stamens ovules ovary (cut in half)

▲ **This picture shows a cross-section of a poppy ovary. Male sex cells from inside the pollen grains travel down to join with female sex cells in the ovules. Fertilization is then complete, and the ovules can begin to develop into seeds.**

Pollen particulars

There is an important reason why each and every kind of flower in the world has its own unique type of pollen. It means that pollen from one plant can fertilize only flowers of the same kind of plant. In other words, only pollen from a flower of the same **species** can grow a tube down into the pistil of another flower. Poppy pollen cannot fertilize a buttercup, honeysuckle, or lily flower. Pollen from the **anther** of a poppy flower can fertilize only the ovule of another poppy flower.

What happens next?

After fertilization, the flower is no longer needed. Almost all the parts of the flower, including the **stamens** and usually the stigma and **style,** wither away. The flower **petals** fade, die, and fall from the plant. The hollow part at the bottom of the flower—the ovary—is all that remains. It slowly forms a **fruit** to protect the seeds that are growing inside.

▲ The red berries on this rose bush are called rosehips. They were once the ovaries of the rose flower. They have enlarged to protect the growing seeds inside.

21

Conifers

Many trees **reproduce** using flowers, just like other flowering plants. However, some trees, called **conifers,** reproduce using **cones.** Most conifers are **evergreen,** with needle-like leaves. Conifer trees include firs, cypresses, pines, cedars, and redwoods.

Male and female cones

Conifers grow two kinds of cones—male and female. The male cone is the smaller and softer of the two. Male cones sometimes look like small **buds** or flowers and are often brightly colored in shades of yellow, purple, or red. When people talk about cones, they usually mean the female cones. When full grown, female cones are much bigger than the male cones and have woody scales.

Male cones usually grow at the tips of branches, where their **pollen** can be caught by the wind. In spring, male cones release vast amounts of yellowish pollen. Most falls to the ground, but some lands on female cones of the same kind of tree. Female cones have two **ovules** on each of their scales with a tiny sticky patch close by. If a pollen grain sticks to this patch, it can form a tube to reach into the ovule. Then the male **sex cell** from the pollen can join with the female sex cell in the ovule to form a **seed.**

◄ The female cones on the European larch (*Larix decidua*) tree are purplish-red at first, becoming hard and woody as the seeds form. Male larch cones are smaller and yellow.

Male cones shrivel and die after they release their pollen. Female cones grow larger after **pollination.** Seeds take one to three years to develop fully. They grow tucked between the scales of the female cones. At first, many female cones are green, and the scales are closed up tight to protect the young seeds. They turn brown and grow bigger and harder as they get older. The seeds inside get larger too.

Releasing the seeds

In some conifers, the scales fall to the ground when the seeds inside are ripe. The seeds are released as the scales fall. Many conifer seeds have papery wings to help them float on the wind far from the parent tree. Cedar cones form a stack of scales that fall off gradually. This ensures that at least some of the seeds fall when the conditions are right for **germination.** In pine trees, the scales open up and the seeds are blown away. Once all the seeds have been released, the cones fall to the ground.

▶ Pine **nuts** are actually the seeds from inside the cone of the Italian stone pine tree (*Pinus pinea*). The seeds are quite big compared to other cone seeds.

Seeds

Most plant **seeds** are no bigger than a grain of sand. Yet everything a new plant needs to start growing is inside these tiny capsules. The giant redwood (*Sequoiadendron giganteum*), which towers 260 feet (80 meters) above the ground, started life as a tiny seed, barely $^8/_{100}$ inch (2 millimeters) long.

Inside a seed

A seed is like a **fertilized** egg. Inside there are two parts—a food supply and an **embryo.** An embryo is like a baby plant. It has the new plant's tiny first leaves and **roots.** The food supply will nourish the young plant with the **energy** it needs to grow in the first days of its life. These inner parts of the seed are wrapped up in a protective **seed coat** that keeps the seed safe until it is ready to **germinate.** When a seed is released from its parent plant, it may be some time before the conditions are right for it to grow. For example, many seeds start to grow only when the temperature is warm enough or if there is enough water. The seed coat keeps the embryo safe from damage and prevents it from drying out until it is ready to germinate.

◄ Seeds in the sandy earth of a dry desert may wait months or even years for rains to come so they can germinate.

Many small seeds

Different plants make different kinds and amounts of seeds. Many plants produce huge numbers of seeds because only a few will manage to grow into new plants. In the tropical forests of Central and South America, trumpet trees can make 900,000 tiny seeds in a season. Even a large oak tree can produce about 50,000 acorns in just one year. Imagine what would happen if all of these seeds grew into trees! In fact, most seeds are eaten by animals or end up in places where they cannot grow. Even if they start to grow, many are soon eaten or trampled on and destroyed by animals. Only a small number survive even one year.

A few large seeds

Some plants produce a few large seeds instead of thousands of tiny ones. Big seeds, such as coconuts, contain large food supplies that help to make sure germination is successful. The food supply gives the seed extra protection so that it has a good chance of surviving, germinating, and growing into a new plant. However, if such a seed fails to germinate, the parent plant may fail to **reproduce.**

▶ **A horsechestnut tree may produce hundreds of seeds each year. Only a few will germinate and grow into new trees.**

Seeds and Fruits

A **fruit** is the part of a plant that develops from the **ovary** of a flower as a **fertilized ovule** ripens into a **seed**. It may take only weeks for the fertilized ovule to develop into a ripe seed. However, some seeds take much longer to grow. For example, the seeds of **conifer** trees take up to three years to develop.

Fruits and the seeds inside them grow and develop at the same time. As the seeds get larger and riper, so do the fruits that hold them. When you see plums on a tree grow bigger and turn from hard and green to soft and purple, it is because the seed inside is gradually growing and ripening as well.

Fleshy and dry fruits

Many plants have fleshy fruits, such as plums and grapes. Some plants form dry fruits. Dry fruits include the **pods** of peas and beans, the hard shell of a hazelnut, and the winged case of a sycamore seed. These have no thick flesh around their seeds.

▲ The flowers of the honesty plant (*Lunaria*) are not especially pretty. Gardeners choose this plant because of its unusual flat, transparent seed pods that look like pearly disks.

Seed dispersal

In addition to protecting the seed as it grows, a plant's fruit has another equally important job to do. When the seed is ripe and ready to leave the parent plant, it is the fruit that helps to carry it away. This movement of the seed away from the plant on which it grew is called seed **dispersal.** Different plants disperse their seeds in a variety of ways. The type of fruit that a plant produces depends on how the seeds are dispersed.

The best place for children to grow up is with their parents, or with other adults who care for them. The same is true for many young animals. Animal parents provide their young with shelter and food and keep them safe until they can take care of themselves. For plants, the opposite is the case. If seeds **germinate** too close to their parent plant, they may not get the light they need to grow. Their small **roots** also will have to fight for space in a patch of ground that is already crowded with the roots of older, stronger plants. A seed's best chance of developing into a healthy new plant is to get far away from its parent plant before it germinates.

► A young **sapling** like this will not survive for long on a forest floor because the light it needs to grow is blocked by the leafy branches of the taller trees.

Seed Dispersal by Wind and Water

From plant to wardrobe

The seeds of cotton plants (*Gossypium*) are carried in the wind by a tuft of white threads. These threads are so long and strong that people can spin them together to form the cotton thread used to make clothes.

▼ **When dandelion seeds land, the parachute breaks off and the seed sinks into the soil, where it waits until it is time for it to germinate.**

Flowering plants that use the wind to **disperse** their **seeds** have special ways to make it successful. Poppies and orchids produce tiny seeds that are light enough to float on the wind when it shakes them from their **fruits.** Some fruits also have special shapes to help them float or fly in the air before they drop to the ground. When these fruits land, they decay and release the seeds into the soil.

Some plants, such as ash trees (*Fraxinus*), have fruits that are shaped like wings that enable them to whirl away in the wind. Maple seeds grow in pairs, and each pair is equipped with a wing-like blade. When the seeds are ripe, the fruit falls from the tree and the wings help them to spin like tiny helicopters in the air.

Some plants, such as dandelions and thistles, grow structures that work like miniature parachutes. Each tiny dandelion seed grows at the end of a thin stalk topped by a circle of white, wispy threads. Even the gentlest of breezes can blow these "parachutes" from the dandelion plant.

Water works

Plants that live near rivers or the sea may use the moving water to scatter their seeds. Some of the seeds that use water dispersal are encased in fruits that contain bubbles of air. These air-filled fruits act like rubber floats, helping the fruits to bob along on the surface of the water. The seeds of water lilies may be dispersed over long distances in this way. They can germinate either in the water or, if they become stranded, on the shore or riverbank.

◄ When a coconut washes up onto a beach, the outer husk decays. The seed gets the **energy** and water it needs to germinate from the supplies it has carried inside it across the sea.

Coconut palm trees (*Cocos nucifera*) often grow on tropical beaches. Their green fruits contain the brown, hairy seeds that are sold in supermarkets. When the seeds are ripe, the fruit falls onto the beach and is washed into the water. The light husk around the coconut helps it to float. The white flesh inside the coconut is stored food, and what we call coconut milk is really water. The coconut floats for sometimes thousands of miles or kilometers across the sea until it is washed up onto another beach. It may then **germinate.** This method of dispersal works so well that coconut palm trees grow on beaches throughout the tropics.

Seed Dispersal by Animals

Millions of animals all over the world help plants disperse their **seeds.** But the animals involved are not even aware they are doing the plants a favor. All they are interested in is making a meal of the **fruits** that the plants have produced.

When a bird picks a fruit such as a berry, it flies off to find a safe place to eat it. Sometimes it drops the berry while in flight; usually it eats only the sweet berry flesh and drops the seed. Either way, the bird has carried the seed a considerable distance and dropped it onto new ground away from its parent plant. Some animals swallow the fruit and seeds together when they eat. The seeds' tough outer coats usually ensure that they will survive intact as they pass through the animal's body. When the seeds are expelled some hours and ideally some miles or kilometers later, they come out coated with their very own supply of **nutrients**—the animal's droppings.

The aardvark farmer

In the heat of the South African desert, the aardvark get its water from the juicy fruit of the gemsbok cucumber (*Acanthosicyos naudinianus*). This suits the cucumber plants perfectly because the aardvark has the habit of burying its droppings and the cucumber seeds below the surface of the ground—out of the heat and at just the right depth for the seeds to germinate!

▶ The fruit of the gemsbok cucumber is a favorite food of the aardvark.

Ready when ripe

Have you ever wondered why fruits do not taste good until they are ripe? While the seed is still growing, fruits are often green, hard, and sour to eat. Some fruits not only taste unpleasant when unripe, but they can also sicken an animal that eats them. Only when the seeds inside are fully developed do the fruits ripen. Apples and cherries change from green to red, and bananas turn yellow. The ripe fruits also give off a tempting scent, advertising to all nearby hungry animals that they are finally ready to eat.

Buried treasure—nuts and seeds

Hungry animals are also responsible for **dispersing** some of the seeds encased in dry fruits. Acorns contain the seeds of the oak tree. Animals such as squirrels collect and carry off many of these **nuts.** They eat some but bury many others, often in open spaces to which they return in winter when food is scarce. However, squirrels, like many nut-hoarding animals, do not have perfect memories, and many nuts are forgotten. In spring, when it is time to grow, many seeds end up in the perfect place for **germination.**

▶ Woodpeckers tuck acorns into specially drilled holes in tree bark as winter food supplies. Many acorns fall to the ground and germinate or are stolen by rodents that carry them off and bury them in spots that are even more suitable for growing.

Other Ways of Dispersing Seeds

Some plants do not rely on animals eating their **fruits** to disperse their **seeds;** they simply hitch a ride to get away. When you come back from a walk in the country, take a look at your clothes. You might find that you are carrying hitchhiking fruits!

Some seeds have fruits covered in long hooks or many tiny spikes that stick to your clothes or to animal fur. You can pick them off with your fingers, but animals have to rub, scratch, or lick them off. If these discarded seeds fall to the ground in a suitable spot, they may be able to **germinate** far away from their parent plant.

Plant inventors

Did you know that when you fasten your shoes or bag with a strip of Velcro™, you have a plant to thank for this useful device? A Swiss inventor named Georges de Mestral came up with the idea of Velcro™ after studying the way plant burrs stuck to his pants. Take a close look at Velcro™. One side is made up of many tiny hooks, just like the surface of a burr. The other side is fuzzy like fur.

▶ Each of the fruits of the burdock plant (*Arctium minus*) is covered in tiny hooks. As an animal brushes past the plant, these fruits cling to the animal's fur and get a free ride to a new place.

Do it yourself!

Some plants are more independent. They do not need the help of wind, water, or animals to scatter their seeds because they are able to do the job of **dispersal** all by themselves. Some of these plants use a type of explosion to blast the seeds far and wide.

Many of the plants that have seeds in **pods,** such as pea and broom plants, release seeds in explosions. The pods of these plants are divided into two sections, which are closed tightly together as the seeds grow. When the seeds are ripe, the pods begin to dry out. In the heat of the sun, they become drier and begin to twist and curl up until the two halves suddenly split open. The sudden blast fires the seeds off in all directions.

A fruit rocket?

The squirting cucumber (*Ecballium elaterium*) uses a very special kind of explosion to discharge its seeds. As the seeds of this plant ripen, the cucumbers that hold them fill with slimy juice. The cucumbers get fatter and fuller until they suddenly shoot off their stalks into the sky, flying through the air like long green missiles. As the fruits travel, the seeds spray onto the ground below, where they may germinate.

Reproducing with Spores

Many plants use **asexual reproduction** to produce offspring. Some of these reproduce using **spores.** Spores are tiny flecks of living material produced by a single plant. When released, the spores are able to grow into a new plant that is identical to the parent plant. Plants that reproduce using spores include ferns and mosses.

Plants form spores in a number of ways. Moss spores are made at the tips of little stalks that grow above the leaves. In ferns, they are found on the underside of the fronds, or leaves, often seen as raised brown patches or spots. Some people mistakenly think these brown patches are a sign of disease. In fact, they are small sacs or packages of tiny spores.

When spores are ripe, spore sacs dry and split open, flinging the spores in all directions. The sacs usually open in warm, dry weather, when the wind can more easily blow the light spores away. Spores may travel very long distances before the wind dies down and they fall to the ground far away from the parent plant. Only spores that land in the right conditions will be able to spring to life. Most spores need to land in damp, shady places in order to **germinate.**

◄ Spores that fall onto unsuitable ground will decay, so mosses and ferns produce millions of spores to ensure that at least some of them land in places where they have a chance of germinating.

The three stages of fern growth

Many spore-producing plants, such as ferns, reproduce through a three-stage process. The spore is the first stage. If a fern spore lands in a damp place, it grows into a thin, heart-shaped flap called a **prothallus.** The prothallus resembles a tiny leaf and is the second stage of reproduction. The prothallus looks nothing like the plant it came from, but a new fern will grow from it.

The prothallus has male and female parts. **Sex cells** from the male parts swim to the female parts of the same or a different prothallus. When a male and a female sex cell join, they begin to form a new fern plant. At first, the baby fern grows on the prothallus. After the new plant grows its own leaves and **roots,** the prothallus dies. This new fern plant is the third and final stage.

A fern's development is complex. It might be helpful to think about how a caterpillar turns into a pupa and a butterfly emerges from the pupa. Similarly, a spore turns into a prothallus, and a fern plant emerges from the prothallus.

▶ **This fern prothallus is about the size of your smallest fingernail. It is the second stage in the life of a fern plant.**

Asexual Reproduction in Plants

Many plants are able to **reproduce** without **seeds** or **spores**. In addition to making seeds, many flowering plants also can use another kind of reproduction to make new versions of themselves. Parts of these plants break off and grow into new, identical copies of their parent. This is called **asexual reproduction.**

Bad weather in spring or summer may prevent flowering plants from forming flowers or keep insect **pollinators** from visiting them. This is not a problem if the plant can reproduce in other ways. There are disadvantages to asexual reproduction, however. Although some plants can make hundreds of seeds, they can make only a few new plants by producing **runners, tubers, bulbs,** or **rhizomes.** Also, because they are identical copies, they may be no better than their parent at surviving in their **habitat.**

The 43,000-year-old parent

Some of the oldest plants in the world reproduce without the use of seeds. There is a **shrub** in Tasmania, Australia, that scientists believe comes from a parent plant that is more than 43,000 years old. King's holly (*Lomatia tasmanica*) spreads by producing new young plants that are individuals identical to itself, or clones. The original parent of this particular plant is long dead, but it lives on in the offspring that grow almost 1 mile (1.5 kilometers) wide and up to 26 feet (8 meters) tall.

◄ Strawberries produce runners that result in identical copies of the parent plant.

Runners

Runners are long **stems** that grow sideways instead of upward from a plant. They reach across the surface of the soil like skinny fingers, searching out new ground. Strawberry plants grow runners. At intervals along the length of a runner, sets of new **roots** and **buds** start to grow and form tiny new strawberry plants. After a short time, these new plants will be big and strong enough to survive on their own. If the runner that attaches them to the parent plant dies or is damaged, the new plants continue growing.

Buttercup plants (*Ranunculus*) also grow runners. They grow one new plant at the tip of a runner, and as soon as it is able to survive on its own, the runner withers away. Once the new buttercup plant is full grown, it grows a runner of its own to produce one new buttercup plant.

The piggyback plant

Have you ever given a friend a piggyback ride? If you ever hear the name *piggyback plant* (*Tolmiea menziesii*), you might be fooled into thinking it got that name by giving other plants a ride. In fact, this plant has a curious way of reproducing. Tiny new plants start to grow from the base of large, older leaves, so it looks just as if they are getting a piggyback ride.

Reproducing from Underground

Some plants **reproduce** by growing new young plants from swollen underground parts. The underground parts are protected from harsh weather by the soil. They often remain unharmed for long periods until the conditions are right for them to grow into new plants.

Tubers and rhizomes

A **tuber** is an underground **stem** or **root** that the plant uses as a food supply. The tuber becomes swollen with food as the plant grows above ground. When a dahlia's (*Dahlia*) flowers and leaves die in fall, the plant lives on underground as a root tuber. In spring, it uses **energy** from the food stored in the tuber to grow new leaves and flowers. Potatoes (*Solanum*) are also stem tubers. If you look at a potato, you can see spots on it. These are **buds,** which we call eyes, and each one can grow into a new potato plant.

A **rhizome** is a special stem that grows sideways, at or just below the soil surface. Rhizomes produce leaves and flowers that rise above the soil and small roots below. These can break free and become separate plants. Some plants also use rhizomes as a place to store food. Plants that grow rhizomes include iris (*Iris*), Canadian wild ginger (*Asarum canadense*), and bracken (*Pteridium aquilinum*).

◄ You can often see the rhizomes of iris plants protruding from the soil at the base of the plant's long, sword-shaped leaves.

▶ These are narcissus and tulip (in center) bulbs. These bulbs can produce flowers early in the year by using their stored food.

Bulbs

Bulbs are underground plant parts. They are made up of layers of thick, fleshy leaves growing around a central bud. Onions are bulbs, and lilies and tulips are flowers that grow from bulbs.

A bulb acts as a winter food supply for the main plant but can grow completely new plants as well. New plants form from small buds that grow from the bulb's side. At first, these buds are tiny, but as they get bigger, they grow their own roots, leaves, stems, and flowers. Eventually, the new bulb and its plant break away from the parent plant to form a separate individual.

Results of reproduction

In this book we have looked at the different ways in which plants reproduce. From **seeds** to **spores, runners** to rhizomes, the plants of the world use various methods of reproduction. Some plants use **asexual reproduction,** which involves only one parent plant. Others use **sexual reproduction,** which requires two parent plants. The methods may be different, but when all plants reproduce they share a common aim—to ensure that they produce offspring that will live on after they have died.

Reproduction is a vital part of the life cycle of every plant. Only by reproducing can plants ensure that their **species** will survive and go on to produce future generations.

Try It Yourself!

Try these experiments and activities to find out more about some of the plant processes you have learned about in this book.

Fruit fun

Looking inside different kinds of **fruit** is a great way of understanding more about where and how **seeds** grow and what makes a fruit.

You will need:

- a selection of different fruits and **nuts** from the supermarket
- paper and pencils
- a knife
- a cutting board
- a nutcracker

Ask an adult to help you slice one of each different kind of fruit in half on the cutting board. Lay them all out on a piece of paper. You should be very careful when opening the nuts in particular (you may need to use a nutcracker).

Make notes or draw a picture of each fruit to show how many seeds it has, where in the fruit they grow, and whether you think it is a fleshy or a hard fruit.

You can also take out the seeds and examine them. If you take their **seed coats** off, you may be able to see inside the seeds.

Seed samplers

You can make attractive displays with seeds that can help you learn about different kinds of seeds.

You will need:

- a collection of seeds. (You can use some seeds taken from fruits, but you can also use seeds you can buy from the store, such as sunflower, sesame, and poppy seeds.)
- glue
- two sheets of thick paper

Using groups of seeds, lay out a design on one of the sheets of paper. You could make a scene, a portrait, or any interesting pattern. When you are happy with your design, cover the other piece of paper with glue and gradually transfer the seeds into position on the new piece of paper. Or you could try covering a piece of paper with glue and pressing it onto your seed pattern to transfer it.

Identifying flower parts

The parts of a flower look different on different kinds of flowers. This activity will help you know what to look for.

You will need:
- three flowers, each of a different type
- paper and pencils
- a knife
- a magnifying glass

Ask an adult to help you cut each of the flowers in half. Lay the flower halves out and see if you can identify the different parts that you can see. You could try writing labels on the paper behind the flower. Label the **stigma, style, ovary, anther, filament, petal,** and **stem.** With a magnifying glass you may also be able to see **pollen** on the anthers and the **ovules** inside the **ovaries.**

Spore prints

You have to wait until you find a fern leaf with brown **spore** sacs on the underside to do this activity, but it is very effective and well worth the wait!

You will need:
- fern leaves that have spore sacs growing on the underside
- sheets of white paper
- a large, heavy book

Lay the fern leaves between two sheets of paper. Make sure the undersides of the leaves are facing downward. Then place this paper "sandwich" underneath the heavy book, and leave it for a few days. Then open the book and very carefully take out the paper, keeping it right side up. When you lift up the fern leaf, you will find that the sacs have pressed into the paper, leaving an interesting outline of the fern leaf.

Looking at Plant Reproduction

Different methods of seed dispersal

There are four main methods that plants use to disperse their **seeds**—wind, water, animal, and explosion.

Wind dispersal

Seeds dispersed by the wind tend to be very small and very light so they can be carried by a breeze when released from their **fruit,** or they have fruits with features that enable them to become airborne.

- *Lightweight seeds:* poppy, orchid
- *Seeds with winged cases*: sycamore, maple, linden, ash
- *Seeds with hairy or feathery fruits:* dandelion, cotton, clematis, artichoke, pussy willow, thistle

Water dispersal

Many plants use water to disperse their seeds. The fruit of water-dispersed seeds need either to be small and light enough to float or to have special features that help them stay on the surface of the water.

- *Small lightweight seeds:* alder, weeping willow.
- *Seeds with buoyant (able to float) fruits:* coconut, lotus, prickly palm

Animal dispersal

Animals may eat soft fruit, and any undigested seeds are passed out in their droppings. Animals store **nuts** that they forget. Other animal-dispersed seeds have fruits with hooks or prickles so that they latch onto the fur of passing animals and hitch a ride to a new spot.

- *Seeds with soft, edible fruits:* elderberry, blackberry, cherry, rosehip
- *Nuts that animals carry away:* acorns, horsechestnut, hazelnut, Brazil nut, almond
- *Seeds with hooked or spiky fruits:* burdock, goosegrass

Explosion dispersal

To scatter the seeds away from the parent plant, some fruits explode when the seeds inside are ripe. Many dry up and shrink so they curl, split, and spray the seeds around.

- *Examples include:* pea, broom, gorse, locust, runner bean

Pollen dispersal

All plants that produce **pollen** use wind, insects, or other animals for **pollination.** Generally, the more drab the flower, the more likely it is a wind-pollinated plant. Animal-pollinated flowers are usually more colorful and strongly scented.

Wind-pollinated plants
- Grasses
- Sedges and rushes
- Conifers, such as pine, spruce, and fir
- Hazel
- Willow
- Poplar
- Walnut
- Oak

- Cedar
- Beet
- Corn
- Sagebrush
- Ragweed
- Russian thistle (tumbleweed)

Insect-pollinated plants
- Pansy
- Tulip
- Rose

- Gardenia
- Squash
- Cucumber
- Cabbage
- Foxglove
- Apple tree
- Orange tree
- Water lily
- Poppy
- Orchid
- Clover
- Honeysuckle

Other animal-pollinated plants
- Saguaro cactus (birds and bats)
- Hibiscus (hummingbirds)
- New Zealand flax (geckos)
- Eucalyptus (opossum)
- Baobab (bat)

Different methods of reproduction

In this book, we talked about the different ways in which plants **reproduce.** Here are lists of the different types of reproduction, with some examples of the plants that use each kind. Remember, some plants may use more than one kind. For example, strawberries make seeds as well as reproducing by making **runners.**

Sexual reproduction (*seeds*)
- Poppy
- Oak tree
- Sunflower
- Horsechestnut
- Rhododendron
- Flax
- Angelica
- Cherry
- Strawberry

Sexual reproduction (*cones*)
- Pine
- Spruce
- Fir
- Redwood
- Cedar
- Cypress

Asexual reproduction (*runners, tubers, rhizomes, bulbs*)
- *Bulbs:* crocus, daffodil, tulip, crocus
- *Runners:* strawberry, cinquefoil, white clover
- *Rhizomes:* iris, bracken, ginger, goldenseal, licorice, valerian
- *Tubers:* potato, dahlia, cassava

Asexual reproduction (*spores*)
- Fern
- Moss
- Liverwort

Glossary

anther   top part of the flower where pollen is found in pollen sacs

asexual reproduction   when a plant reproduces by creating another plant from a part of itself

bud   swelling on a plant stem of tiny, young overlapping leaves or petals and other parts of a flower, ready to burst into bloom

bulb   underground bud protected by layers of thick, fleshy leaves. An onion is a kind of bulb.

cells   building blocks of living things, so small they can be seen only with a microscope. Some microbes consist of only a single cell, but most plants and animals are made up of millions or billions of cells.

cluster   group of flowers growing together

cone   form of dry fruit produced by conifer trees in which seeds develop. Cones are often egg-shaped and are made up of many overlapping scales.

conifer   kind of tree that has cones and needlelike leaves

disperse   scatter or spread widely

embryo   very young plant contained in a seed

energy   ability in living things to do what they need to in order to live and grow. Plants and animals get the energy they need from their food.

evergreen   type of plant that does not lose all its leaves at once, but loses some leaves and grows new ones all year round

fertilize   when a male sex cell and a female sex cell join together and begin to form a seed

filament   part of a flower that holds up the anther

fruit   part of a plant that contains and protects its seeds

genes   set of instructions that control how an organism looks and how it will survive, grow, and change through its life

germinate   when a seed starts to grow

habitat   place where plants and animals live

honeyguides   special markings on flowers that lead insect pollinators to the nectar. They are near the flower's reproductive parts to ensure that the insect receives or delivers pollen.

nectar   sugary substance plants make to attract insects

nut   kind of hard fruit. The hard shell of a nut is the fruit. The inner part, which we sometimes eat, is the seed.

nutrient   chemical that nourishes plants and animals

nutritious   healthful, or full of nutrients

organism living thing, such as bacteria, algae, plants, and animals

ovary rounded bottom part of the pistil. The ovary is the part of the flower that may turn into a fruit containing the seeds.

ovule plant's female sex cell. Ovules are found inside the ovary and can become seeds after they have joined with a male sex cell from a pollen grain.

peat bog area of marshy ground formed from the partially decayed remains of a plant

petals colored parts of a flower

photosynthesis process by which plants make their own food using water, carbon dioxide, and energy from sunlight

pistil name for the female parts of a flower. The ovary, style, and stigma together make up a pistil.

pollen tiny, dustlike particles produced by a flower that contain the plant's male sex cells

pollinate/pollination when pollen travels from the anthers of one flower to the stigma of the same or a different flower

pollinator insect or animal that carries pollen from one flower to another

prothallus tiny, plantlike organism that grows from a spore. A fern prothallus can produce a new fern plant.

reproduce/reproduction when a living thing produces young like itself

rhizome special kind of stem that grows under the ground instead of up in the air

roots plant parts that grow under the ground. Roots hold a plant in place and absorb water and nutrients from the soil.

runner long, thin stem that grows sideways from a plant. New plants can grow from runners.

sapling young tree

seed part of the plant that contains the beginnings of a new plant.

seed coat tough, outer skin of a seed that protects the tiny, new plant inside that is waiting to grow

sex cell type of cell that plants and animals make in their sexual parts. When a male sex cell and a female sex cell join, they can form a seed.

sexual reproduction when a plant reproduces by joining a male and a female sex cell

shrub plant with a woody stem that usually does not grow above 20 feet (6 meters)

species kind of living thing

spores tiny particles, usually containing a single cell, that are released by plants

stamen male part of a flower that produces pollen

stem part of a plant that holds it upright and supports its leaves and flowers

stigma female part of the flower that receives pollen in the process of pollination. Stigmas are usually found at the top of a stalk.

style stalk that holds up the stigma of a flower and attaches the stigma to the ovary

tuber short, thick underground stem. New tubers and new plants can grow from the buds on a tuber.

ultraviolet kind of light that insects can see and humans cannot

Find Out More

Books

Bailey, Jill. *Plants and Plant Life*. Danbury, Conn.: Grolier Educational, 2000.

Burnie, David. *The Plant*. New York: Dorling Kindersley, 2000.

Esparza, June. *Tiny Seedlings...Their Journey*. San Antonio, Tex.: Thoughts in Motion, 1999.

Joly, Dominique, et al. *How Does Your Garden Grow? Be Your Own Plant Expert*. New York: Sterling Publishing Company, 2000.

Legg, Gerald. *The World of Plant Life*. Milwaukee: Gareth Stevens, Inc., 2002.

Pascoe, Elaine. *Seeds Travel*. Milwaukee: Gareth Stevens, Inc., 2002.

Conservation sites

Center for Plant Conservation
P.O. Box 299
St. Louis, MO 63166-0299
Tel: (314) 577-9450

Lady Bird Johnson Wildflower Center
4801 La Crosse Avenue
Austin, TX 78739-1702
Tel: (512) 292-4200

New England Wild Flower Society
180 Hemenway Road
Framingham, MA 01701
Tel: (508) 877-7630

California Native Plant Society
1722 J Street, Suite 17
Sacramento, CA 95814
Tel: (415) 970-0394

The State Botanical Garden of Georgia
2450 S. Milledge Avenue
Athens, GA 30605
Tel: (706) 542-6448

Places to visit

Many museums, arboretums (botanical garden devoted to trees) and botanic gardens are fascinating places to visit. You could try:

The New York Botanical Garden
Bronx River Parkway at Fordham Road
Bronx, NY 10458
Tel: (718) 817-8700

Denver Botanic Gardens
1005 York Street
Denver, CO 80206
Tel: (720) 865-3500

Atlanta Botanical Garden
1345 Piedmont Avenue NE
Atlanta, GA 30309
Tel: (404) 876-5859

Garfield Park Conservatory
300 North Central Park Ave.
Chicago, IL 60624-1996
Tel: (312) 746-5100

University of California Botanical Garden
200 Centennial Drive
Berkeley, CA 94720
Tel: (510) 643-2755

Missouri Botanical Garden
P.O. Box 299
St. Louis, MO 63166-0299
Tel: (314) 577-9400

Index

48